I think you are already in the meshes of the net! The Holy Spirit is after you. I doubt if you'll get away!

C.S. Lewis to Sheldon Vanauken
A Severe Mercy

Dedication

To my youngest brother Michael,
who loved the number five.

Contents

1   Quote, C.S. Lewis

5   Introduction

6   *Jericho*

8   **The Son for the Gates**

24   Notes

31   Discussion Questions

33   Prayer

34   *Joppa*

36   **Elijah's Mantle**

58   Monsters from the Deep

60   Notes

66   Discussion Questions

67   Prayer

68   Acknowledgments and Attributions

70   Quote, C.S. Lewis

Introduction

When I was a teenager, I would often think to myself that I didn't like the ending of a television episode I'd just watched. So I'd go to bed restructuring the storyline in my mind. I'd try to analyse where the plot started going wrong and, from there, I'd devise a new finale. Sometimes this took more than a single evening's mental exercise. It would be days before I found a way to bring about a satisfactory resolution to the story.

I never admitted that sometimes, when I was supposed to be paying attention in class, I was day-dreaming up a happily-ever-after to a story that didn't reach the potential I'd have liked.

Now very recently it occurred to me that God does just this. Not the day-dreaming part, of course, but the remaking of storylines.

When Jesus heals history, it's possible to see the unfolding of an ancient plot, the beginning of the re-enactment of a dramatic episode from one of the pages of history, and then — ah, then, a changepoint. A critical departure from the old narrative, a reworked climax, a fresh finale. Jesus resolves the endings into lovely, wondrous, captivating wrap-ups.

In other books in this series, we've seen how He chooses some of the most traumatic events in the history of the land and unveils a new ending for them. Highlights include his visits to Emmaus and Sychar, as well as the journey from Bethany-beyond-the-Jordan to Bethany near Jerusalem.

In this book, we'll see a double healing of people and landscape at Jericho. It's one of those healing bundles Jesus specialised in — He'd take on two or more tragedies simultaneously and bind them up together in one healing. He had an amazing capacity to reach deep into the past to heal its wounds and to redeem wasted time.

The second section of this book looks at something slightly different. It's about how Jesus set up the circumstances for a healing of history that actually occurred after He ascended to heaven. This was an event for which He was not physically present.

And so it speaks to us in our own time of the people, places and power He has set in train for us so we can fulfil those healings of history He wants us to accomplish for the advancement of His kingdom.

May you know His purpose in history for yourself and for your nation.

Anne Hamilton
Seventeen Mile Rocks
July 2022

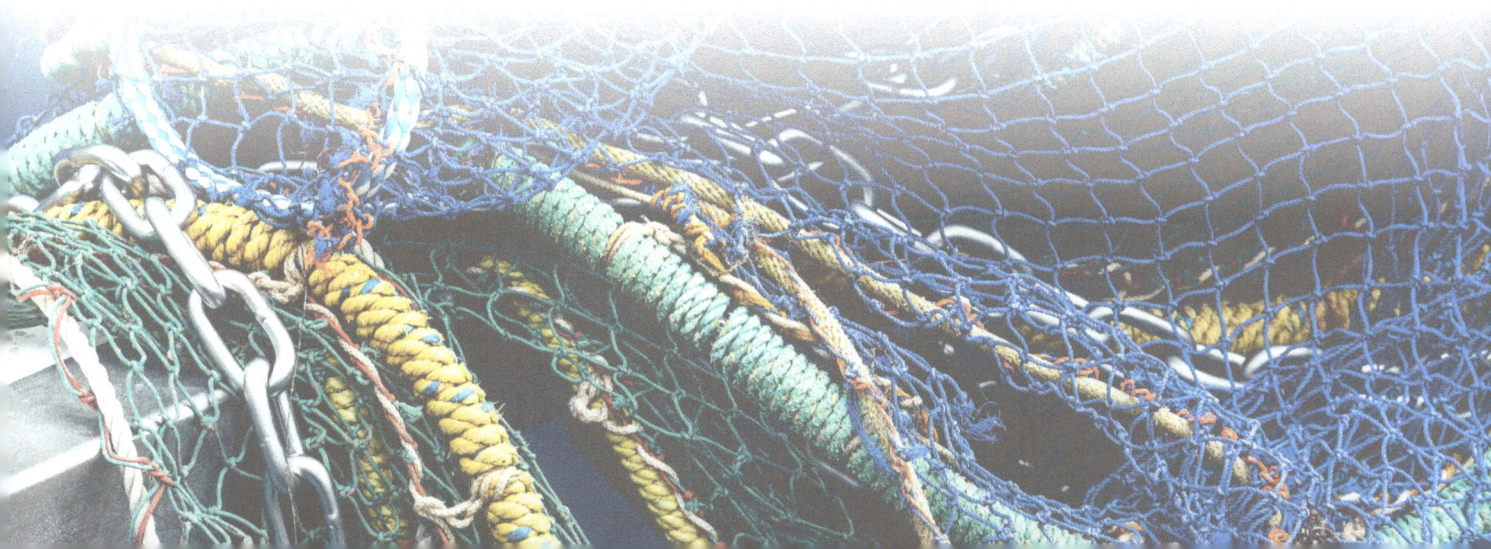

JERICHO

---— Luke 19:1-3 BSB ———

Then Jesus entered Jericho and was passing through. And there was
a man named Zacchaeus, a chief tax collector, who was very wealthy.
He was trying to see who Jesus was…

In Ahab's time, Hiel of Bethel rebuilt Jericho.
He laid its foundations at the cost of his firstborn son Abiram,
and he set up its gates at the cost of his youngest son Segub,
in accordance with the word of the Lord spoken by Joshua.

1 Kings 16:23 NIV

Mark 10:46 NIV

Then they came to Jericho.
As Jesus and His disciples, together with a large crowd,
were leaving the city, a blind man, Bartimaeus
(which means *son of Timaeus*), was sitting by the roadside begging.

THE SON FOR THE GATES

A narrative retelling of the healing of Jericho from the perspective of a local tax-collector.

No matter where you go in Jericho, there's a priest to remind you of your shortcomings. 'Shorty, Shorty,' they'd hiss to attract my attention and lecture me on the evils of money. 'Dishonest wealth will dwindle, but what is earned through hard work will be multiplied.'[1]

So, many thousands of times I have been told, said Solomon, son of David. *If I had a shekel for every time... no, stupid, stupid thought. Don't go there.*

There are twelve thousand priests in Jericho,[2] at least according to rumour. All of them ready to be called up the mountain at a moment's notice. The number is exaggerated, I assure you. Believe me, I know. I have to account for them all — those who pay tax and those who, for whatever reason, are exempt.

Still, if you include in the count the priests and Levites from Ein Karem,[3] Bethany,[4] Anathoth[5] and Emmaus, then twelve thousand would probably come close. But those villages are well outside my jurisdiction. True, I knew most of the priests from those localities during their younger days and none of us, I guessed, have fond memories of each other.

As the priests get older and the once-in-a-lifetime lot still hasn't favoured them, one of two things tends to happen. The dream of their single day ministering in the Temple dies. They sell up and

---

1.
Proverbs 13:11 BSB

2.
Groups in the Gospels (1), see: believersmagazine.com

3.
Traditional home of Zachary and Elizabeth and birthplace of John the Baptist.

4.
Residence of Lazarus, Martha and Mary.

5.
Residence of Jeremiah the prophet.

move to a cheaper neighbourhood. Often in the Galilee or down towards Gaza. Or else the dream doesn't die. Then, in stupid, stupid undying hope, they decide the road up to Jerusalem is getting steeper by the year and they rent a pitifully small room as close to the Temple as they can afford. Sometimes their families support them and they manage to pay for a tiny garden as well. But more often than not, some rich Pharisee takes advantage of their pious wish to be ready at a moment's notice when the call finally comes. But for most of them it never does. There are too many of them for Temple service but they are too proud to abandon the dream. Most of them die in desperate poverty.[6]

That brings me to why I first became interested in Jesus: some Pharisees and a Levite. I'd heard the swirling rumours, but dismissed them. People will believe stupid, stupid things when they're chafing under a corrupt government.

Anyway, these Pharisees had collared a young man from a priestly family — Nahum, son of Isaac and Leah. Clearly they'd offered him enough financial incentive to overcome any misgivings about approaching me in public. 'D-do they p-p-pay t-taxes?' he stuttered as the Pharisees looked on from a safe distance.

'Do who pay taxes?' I barked at him. More loudly than necessary. Because I liked Nahum and I didn't want to think half the town would never speak to him again because he'd been seen whispering

6.
Because there were so many priests, their names were drawn by lot for Temple service. If they received a call at all, it was usually only for a single day.

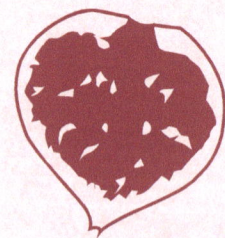

to me. I could tell the Pharisees had targeted Nahum because of his threadbare coat and tattered sandals. But I knew Nahum. He'd share his good fortune with those families who were even poorer. Which didn't mean I wasn't going to have to tax him anyway.

'How much did they give you?' I muttered.

'T-ten shekels.'

I frowned at him. A hundred times too much. Then I realised. *Stupid, stupid,* I thought. *That's the bribe for me.* It was kind of flattering to think they thought I couldn't be bought for less. 'Hand them over,' I demanded.

He didn't hesitate. I made a show of counting it and managed to slip five of the shekels back to him. 'Don't tell anyone,' I muttered under my breath. 'Or I'll take the rest.'

He didn't even smile. Smart boy.

'S-so do they pay taxes?' His nervousness was leaving. The stuttering was less.

'Who?' I barked again.

'The rabbi. And His disciples. Do they pay taxes when they come through Jericho?'

What a stupid, stupid question. 'Of course they do,' I snapped. 'Everyone does. Like it or not.'

'At full rate?'

'Of course full rate.' I wasn't pretending to shout any longer. I was getting angry. Were these Pharisees setting me up? If the Romans suspected I wasn't doing my job, I'd be lucky to stay alive past lunch time.

'No discounts for old friends in the business?' Nahum persisted.

I lowered my voice. 'Are they crazy?' I asked. 'Whoever heard of a rabbi who was once a tax-collector?'

'Not the rabbi,' Nahum said. 'One of his students.'

That was almost as incredible. But then, a bubble of memory floated towards the surface of my mind. *A rumour about…*

'Matthew, from Galilee.' Nahum supplied the name that was trapped within the bubble.

I understood. Every tax-collector from Dan to Beersheba had heard of Matthew,[7] the disciple of rabbi Jesus. He'd done the unthinkable. He was a Levite who, to support his parents and brothers and sisters, had sacrificed any hope of ever serving in the Temple by taking a job as a tax-collector. He'd gone from the heights to the depths. I knew what they'd have said to him. I heard it every day. Even more often than Solomon's line about dishonest wealth. *No hope of salvation for you, Shorty.*

7.
See Matthew 9:9–13

8.
See: randomgroovybiblefacts.com/up-a-tree.html

Nahum's parents prayed for me. I'd turned on them once when they told me so and snarled, 'Don't you know that men like me can never inherit salvation?' I suspected half Jericho prayed for a fatal accident for me.

'We pray for your safety,' his mother said.

It would never do to thank them.

Another time his father commented, while paying taxes, 'I had a vision of you once while studying the Torah. Did you know our first parents hid in the tree in the middle of the garden after eating the forbidden fruit? That is what the Word says: in the midst of the tree.[8] They must have climbed it and fashioned their fig-leaf garments there. And apparently they were still perched up the Tree of the Knowledge of Good and Evil while they spoke to The Name, blessed be He.'

'I don't take payment in stories.'

'Nor should you. I am telling you my vision because it concerns you. I saw you climbing a fig tree. But it was not to hide from The Name. It was to watch for His coming.' A twinkle appeared in Isaac's eye. 'No doubt it was to assess His taxable income.'

I laughed. More to cover how much I was touched by their prayers and concern than in response to the joke. 'How much could I charge the King of the Universe?' I mused. 'Should I demand an accounting of Him for all the Romans have taken from us?'

As soon as the words were out of my mouth, I knew fear. *Stupid, stupid remark*. The sort that, if repeated, could get me killed.

Isaac just nodded. 'And that is why we pray safety for you,' he said.

As I remembered the kindness of Nahum's parents, I felt a spike of rage at the questioning of the Pharisees, and at involving the boy in their manipulations. With a growl, I sent him off and stalked back to the tax booths at the gates. Somewhere there, amongst my own subordinates, would be a source of information about Matthew of Galilee. Unless the rabbi's band travelled through Samaria or took the long route to Jerusalem down by the Way of the Sea, they'd have had to have come through Jericho every festival time. One of my assistants surely had to be able to recognise them on sight.

On my way to the booths, it dawned on me that I should know more about this rabbi Jesus than I did. A holy man travelling with a band of disciples: usually they were the trouble-makers at the gates. Arguing the theology of tithes and taxes, holding up the queues, expecting exemptions, wheedling and wheeling — that was the usual way. But no one had ever called me to break up any impending unrest involving this group. Surely one of the juniors hadn't just let them through — merely to keep the peace?

And tumbling into the midst of these thoughts was the picture of Adam up the fig tree. It wouldn't be chased away. Adam — the name means *man*. As mine also means *man*. Yes, slightly different nuances: man as inspirited dirt compared to man as a vessel of memory, but still *man*. Adam was the guardian,[9] the watcher, the steward of the garden, the one exiled beyond the gates.[10]

And I was exiled. Not beyond the gates. But *at* the gates. That's where I stationed my booths, allowing no one entry until they paid their taxes or showed evidence they had.

But garden? Perhaps. I guessed Jericho could strictly be classed as a garden. It is famous throughout the world for its date palms, persimmon groves, and wide variety of sweet citrus. And of course renowned for its ravishing fragrances. Cleopatra of Egypt so coveted those divinely scented persimmon plantations that Mark Antony gave the entire city to her as a gift. Then she leased it to Herod the

9.
In Genesis 2:15, the Lord's command to 'keep' the garden as a shomer is to fulfil the tasks of guardian, watcher and regent.

10.
Genesis 3:23

11.
See jewishvirtuallibrary.org

The fig tree forms its early fruit; the blossoming vines spread their fragrance.

Arise, come, my darling; my beautiful one, come with me.

Song of Solomon 2:13 NIV

Great for an extortionate sum — half his annual revenue from the rest of Judea. Of course, he got it all in the end — and built his own gardens there. But beautiful as they were, they weren't Eden.[11]

And I wasn't Adam. Old Isaac had at least suggested a different ending to my story. But he was wrong. Totally wrong. I don't watch for God. I gave that up long ago. There's only so much frayed hope the human spirit can cling to before it snaps.

I thought of Matthew of Galilee; Matthew who had once been a Levite. I understood him. I understood why he'd stopped hoping; and I understood why he'd snatched a chance to hope again. He'd learn. It's useless. There's no going back. There's no repentance for the likes of us.

It turned out that my manager Joachim knew the entire group from Galilee. They'd come through his booth regularly on their travels. I ordered him to close his booth and took him aside, causing no end of consternation amongst the staff. But I told him I was suspicious of a bunch of Pharisees, looking to make trouble that in some way involved the Galilean rabbi. And I said I wanted to head it off before it involved our business. That explanation would be enough to quell unrest amongst the other assistants. Keep them alert, too, I expected.

'You wouldn't spot Jesus or His disciples easily, boss,' Joachim said. 'They don't look the part, for a start. No serious faces. No long tassels on their prayer shawls. Quite a few women in the group. High class women, too. There's one who always hides her face but I saw her once, as I was just coming off duty, and she was ducking into the old winter palace through the back garden. That's how I rumbled the group. Did a bit of digging and discovered she was the wife of Chuza, Herod's steward. So I know we don't want trouble with Herod Antipas, boss, and that's why I don't give them trouble.' He sniffed, as if he thought maybe I thought he wasn't giving sufficient reason for his lenient behaviour. 'That, and they don't give me trouble. Always have the exact money ready, no quibbling about change. Smooth transaction, every time.'

'There's a former tax-collector amongst them.'

'So I heard.'

'What's He look like?'

'Jesus?' Joachim shrugged. 'A man.'

Adam? Did he say *'Adam'*? A stupid, stupid quip occurred to me. 'He like figs?'

'Heard that He cursed a fig tree and it died.'[12]

I thought about that for half a minute. 'Send word to me the next time you see them coming,' I commanded. And I went off in search of those Pharisees with the deep pockets. Spending ten shekels for information indicated how serious their intent was.

I thought it would be a Sabbath or two before I got news from Joachim so I headed for the tavern and hid in a dark corner to listen and think about figs. Eat figs too, as a matter of fact. I was actually trying to collect information from conversations about Jesus but figs kept intruding into my thoughts.

Miracle-worker. *Figs*.

Messiah. *Figs*.

Messenger of the Most High. *Figs*.

I gathered from the conversations that people weren't sure which label to attach to Jesus but they knew the court of the Sanhedrin was against Him so that didn't exactly decrease his popularity.

I'd been there less than an hour when Nahum dashed in, seeking me. 'Joachim said you wanted to know when a certain person arrived in Jericho with His entourage.'

The boy had style. I'd give him that. You'd think he was talking about the Emperor Tiberius the way he spoke.

'He's here?' I asked.

'With a crowd of thousands.'

'What?!' Joachim had given me the impression Jesus came and went unannounced. Discreetly. Quietly. 'Smooth transaction' as I recalled.

'He's healed Bartimaeus,' Nahum said.

'Impossible!' I leapt up. 'It's a publicity stunt.'

12.
I have taken some artistic licence with this statement as the cursing of the fig tree seems to have happened later, after Jesus completed the healings at Jericho.

'I saw it happen.' Nahum's face was inscrutable.

Me, I'd always been an expert on expressions, but I couldn't penetrate this one. 'How?'

Bartimaeus was a feature of the old town. He had his favourite spot and he'd be there, every day, by the wayside, begging bowl out, pestering the pilgrims.

Nahum's expression became even more unreadable. 'He simply called out to Jesus. "Son of David," that's what he cried. People kept telling him to be quiet but, you know him, that was an invitation to shout even louder. "Son of David, have mercy on me!"[13] And when Jesus heard him, He summoned him over. So he left his coat and went up to Jesus and that was it. He was healed, right then and there.' An abrupt smile appeared on Nahum's face. 'He's following Jesus now, coming this way.'

It'd be madness at the tax booths, with thousands trying to push through the gates into the new town. There'd be no containing the crush.

'I need to go,' Nahum said. 'Find a good vantage point. I want to see the second healing.'

13.
Mark 10:48 NIV

'What second healing?' I'd heard enough about Jesus in the tavern talk to know He wouldn't restrict Himself to just two. Or would He? Maybe He'd do one for the old city, one for the new. 'I thought He healed everyone who asked.'

'So it's said.' Nahum's nod was thoughtful. 'But don't you see? This is not about the healing of the people, it's about the healing of the city. He's undoing the curse of Joshua.'

'What curse of Joshua?'

'Don't you know the prophets and the histories?'

'Proverbs of Solomon are my specialty. Particularly the ones about money.'

Nahum shook his head and sighed. 'After the battle of Jericho and the destruction of the city, Joshua who commanded the forces of Israel, prophesied over the ruins: "Cursed before the Lord is the man who rises up and builds this city Jericho; with the loss of his firstborn he shall lay its foundation, and with the loss of his youngest son he shall set up its gates." [14] That came to pass in the days when King Ahab and Queen Jezebel ruled in Samaria. Hiel of Bethel[15] rebuilt Jericho — laying its foundation at the cost of his first son Abarim and setting up the gates at the cost of his youngest son Segub.'

'I'm impressed, Nahum. With your knowledge of Scripture, you should be a Levite.'

14.
Joshua 6:26 NASB

15.
1 Kings 16:34

He ignored my sarcasm. 'Bar-tim-ae-us.' He said it with slow emphasis. 'Don't you see? Bar: *son*. Timaeus: from *lay a foundation*. Bartimaeus: *son of the foundation*. Jesus has done a healing for the curse of the firstborn. Jesus is the new Joshua — and instead of cursing the city, He's restoring it. That's why there's got to be a second healing. The one for the son at the gates.'

I'd never realised before that the boy was a mystic. Healing for the city. *What a stupid, stupid idea.*

'In the Torah,' Nahum went on, 'it says that towns like this are to remain a ruin forever.[16] So great is their defilement on our nation. But we have not only rebuilt Jericho and inhabited it, our priests prefer to reside here.' His smile was abrupt, his face a picture of bliss. 'Jesus is removing the ancient stain. And we are here to watch this history-making moment.'

I was persuaded. I wanted to check out the man who could excite this young Levite to raptures. And I wanted to know if Bartimaeus' eyesight was still intact.

The tavern was empty. We'd already wasted too much time in conversation. Going outside, I could see rooftops and doorways crowded with people and burly men shouldering and jostling their way up stairways already crammed with onlookers. 'Too late,' I said.

'I know a place,' Nahum said, pulling me by the elbow. I wondered at his touch. Surely he'd have to isolate for a week after contacting someone as unclean as a tax-collector.

'No one will be there,' he went on. 'The wall of the old palace. Herod's winter garden.'

'Don't be ridiculous.'

'Don't worry. It's got a great view. And the wall's not unclean. Only Herod is. *Was*, I mean.' He flicked me a smile. 'Maybe I shouldn't say even that. Do not speak ill of the dead.'

As we hurried through the throngs lining the streets, I considered the prospect of the wall. The sheer boldness of sitting there might just mean we'd get away with it. 'You've got a ladder?' I asked.

16.
Deuteronomy 13:12–17

'There's a convenient tree.'

'I don't want to know how you know all this.'

'You suspect me of thieving from Herod's garden?' Nahum stopped a moment, affronted. 'Gleaning, that's what it's called. Perfectly within the ancient law.'[17]

The crowds had thinned considerably. But I knew it was only temporary. We reached the tree and Nahum was up it in a moment, reaching back down to help me into the first fork. If I had had any knowledge of botany, I might have refused then and there. But, back then, to me a tree was a tree. I had no idea I was climbing a fig, of all species.

A sycamore, to be exact. A tree whose fruit was pig food. I knew about the pig food aspect, but not that the tree was a fig. In retrospect, I should have suspected why there was such a tree outside Herod's garden. Someone's idea of a joke. A play on that quip of old Augustus Caesar: *it is better to be Herod's pig than his son.* Three of his sons had been executed on suspicion of plotting against their father — his firstborn Antipater just five days before Herod's own death.

Also in retrospect, I should have suspected Nahum's motives. He was far too accommodating. He shimmied along a branch to make room for me as the street began to fill with people. Craning their necks, they lined the walls three deep. At last I saw a sudden surge rounding the nearest corner. The hubbub was intense.

Nahum was on the wall, his hand out to me. But I decided not to move. I could see some of the crowd below, eyeing me with a calculating look. I realised I might just present a prospect a little too tempting. How easy it would be to push a hated tax-collector off a branch. I was safe and snug where I was. I settled deeper into the tree and peered down through the leaves, straining for my first glimpse of the one who was the people's darling.

17.
Leviticus 23:22

I could see why the Pharisees hated Him. The pulse of humanity throbbing down the street was almost riotous. The noise — incredible and joyous.

Then the crowd stopped moving. The roar of voices subsided. Slowly. Very slowly. It was a full minute before all movement stopped and sound ceased.

Silence.

Broken only by the cry of a lone eagle echoing up from the Jordan Valley.

I didn't need anyone to point out Jesus because He was looking right into my hiding place. 'Zacchaeus,' He said, 'hurry and come down, for today I must stay at your house.'[18]

How does He know my name? That's what I was thinking. *Stupid, stupid question.* If He can heal a blind man, how much easier is it to know a tax-collector's name?

I climbed down, glaring at Nahum the whole time. His grin was so infernal I realised he'd set me up. 'Fig tree?' I muttered.

He nodded.

'Be at my house,' I hissed. 'Now.'

'Wouldn't miss it for the world,' he laughed, loud enough for the whole crowd to hear.

18. Luke 19:5 NASB

In that moment, it dawned on me: Nahum was a follower of Jesus. And he had so desperately, desperately, desperately wanted to introduce me to his rabbi that he didn't care who saw him talking to me or touching me.

What kind of healing did he anticipate out of this day? Was it the one for the son of the gates? Or for the son who hid in the tree? Was it for the son in exile? Or for the son who believed he was beyond salvation?

I was going to disappoint them. I knew it. Nahum's compassion was futile. I was unworthy of his risks. Jesus' healing was not for me. If the rabbi came to my house and accepted my hospitality, He would become my covenant defender.[19] I couldn't allow that to happen. He was obviously a good man. I couldn't despoil and contaminate His ministry by allowing Him to cross my threshold.

I heard the crowd's murmur. I could imagine the critics. 'He has gone in to be the guest of a man who is a sinner!'[20]

I was trying to think of a way to extricate us all from this situation. But… there was a troubling image in my mind's eye. I kept seeing the face of Jesus as He looked up into that fig tree. And I felt as if I was in another age, the time of long ago, and I was indeed Adam looking down through the fig leaves into the face of God. Into the face of Love itself.

And all God wanted was for me to say I was sorry. Adam hadn't done that — just tried to shift blame and responsibility. Could I say what Adam had failed to say?

Yet words would not be enough. I grasped Nahum's sleeve. 'Proverbs of Solomon do not discuss repentance,' I whispered. 'What does the Torah say?'

'For your situation, it's tough.' The boy sounded both surprised and sad. 'It's meant as a deterrent, you know. On stealing alone, it's repayment four times over.'

I sighed. Could I do what Adam had failed to do? Could I do the impossible and not only say sorry to God but mean it? Could I enact the apology with fourfold restitution?

As we reached the gate of my house, I made my decision.

19.
Ancient rites of hospitality involved far more than the simple sharing of a meal. To 'pass over' a threshold meant an implicit acceptance of a covenant of mutual defence. To 'strike' or 'dash the foot' against the cornerstone on the threshold was to refuse such a covenant. See: Anne Hamilton, *God's Pageantry: The Threshold Guardians and the Covenant Defender*, Armour Books 2015

20.
Luke 19:7 NASB

Notes

As Jesus approached Jericho, a blind man was sitting by the roadside begging. When he heard the crowd going by, he asked what was happening. They told him, 'Jesus of Nazareth is passing by.'

He called out, 'Jesus, Son of David, have mercy on me!'

Those who led the way rebuked him and told him to be quiet, but he shouted all the more, 'Son of David, have mercy on me!'

Jesus stopped and ordered the man to be brought to Him. When he came near, Jesus asked him, 'What do you want Me to do for you?'

'Lord, I want to see,' he replied.

Jesus said to him, 'Receive your sight; your faith has healed you.' Immediately he received his sight and followed Jesus, praising God. When all the people saw it, they also praised God.

Jesus entered Jericho and was passing through. A man was there by the name of Zacchaeus; he was a chief tax collector and was wealthy. He wanted to see who Jesus was, but because he was short he could not see over the crowd. So he ran ahead and climbed a sycamore-fig tree to see Him, since Jesus was coming that way.

When Jesus reached the spot, He looked up and said to him, 'Zacchaeus, come down immediately. I must stay at your house today.' So he came down at once and welcomed Him gladly.

All the people saw this and began to mutter, 'He has gone to be the guest of a sinner.'

But Zacchaeus stood up and said to the Lord, 'Look, Lord! Here and now I give half of my possessions to the poor, and if I have cheated anybody out of anything, I will pay back four times the amount.'

Jesus said to him, 'Today salvation has come to this house, because this man, too, is a son of Abraham. For the Son of Man came to seek and to save the lost.'

Luke 18:35–19:10 NIV

Jericho, said to be the oldest city in the world, is located in the Jordan Valley — within part of the great rift that extends from Lebanon in the north through to southern Africa. A steep road to the west leads from the valley floor up to the hills of Jerusalem while a much gentler descent heads southeast towards the Dead Sea, the lowest point on the earth's surface.

Jericho's modern name in Arabic is ʿArīḫā', *fragrant*, deriving from a Canaanite root word, 'Reaḫ'. The Hebrew name, 'Yeriḫo', possibly points to another Canaanite word 'Yareaḫ', *moon*, from the name of the lunar deity, Yarikh.

Of the many battles recounted in Scripture, the taking of Jericho by the Israelites under Joshua is amongst the most memorable. No frontal attack, no siegeworks, no secret access, no clever ambushes, no inside insurrection — none of the usual strategies of combat. Not even a battle of champions as was to occur when David faced Goliath.

Instead, after meeting the Commander of the Armies of the Lord on the plains outside the city, Joshua begins the most unusual campaign in the history of warfare. A silent march of the army around the city for six days. Then, a seven times encirclement accompanied by the blowing of ram's horns, culminating in a long final blast that was a signal for the army to shout. As the walls fell, the warriors were to attack.

Nothing and no-one was spared. Everything was destroyed.[21] When it was over, Joshua pronounced a curse:

> Cursed before the Lord is the man who rises up
> and rebuilds this city, Jericho;
> at the cost of his firstborn he will lay its foundations;
> at the cost of his youngest he will set up its gates.[22]

Such a deterrent suggests Joshua was trying to protect his contemporaries from defilement of a major order on the land. The command to utterly destroy Jericho and the warning about rebuilding it harks back to Lord's instruction to Moses about cities contaminated by worship of the dark spirit Belial:

21.
One of the soldiers, Achan, did retrieve a beautiful imported robe, a wedge of gold and a stack of silver coins but they were later disposed of when his transgression was discovered.

22.
Joshua 6:26 BSB

> You must certainly put to the sword all who live in that town. You must destroy it completely, both its people and its livestock. You are to gather all the plunder of the town into the middle of the public square and completely burn the town and all its plunder as a whole burnt offering to the Lord your God. That town is to remain a ruin forever, never to be rebuilt, and none of the condemned things are to be found in your hands.[23]

It was about five hundred years before Hiel of Bethel decided to take the risk that Joshua's curse had dissipated. But it was revealed as true prophecy when the cost of laying the foundation was his firstborn son Abiram, and that for the gates was his youngest son Segub. This seems to suggest, since evil retains its character in a locality over time unless it's dealt with, that the original inhabitants of Jericho worshipped Belial and practised human sacrifice, particularly children.

Literature from the time after the return from exile in Babylon indicates Belial was, in that later era, a name given to the leader of a group of spirits who descended to earth to seek human women as mates.[24] The hybrid angelic-human offspring of these Watchers were regarded as malevolent giants by the Israelites but were revered as superhuman culture heroes amongst other nations. Statuettes of these superhumans, called 'watchers', were buried at thresholds — in foundations and under doorways and gates — as protective talismans.

Blood, however, speaks. In a way that clay figurines do not. The people of Israel, copying

23.
Deuteronomy 13:15–17 NIV

24.
Genesis 6:2–4 alludes to this event.

the practices of the nations around them, eventually came to sacrifice their own flesh and blood to become the most effective threshold watchers. It is implied that this is what Hiel of Bethel did — that it wasn't until the apostasy during the reign of Ahab and Jezebel that such an unthinkable act was again a possibility. Only when Moloch worship and child sacrifice became routine could a man choose a plot of ground over the lives of his children.

Hiel's sons, Abiram and Segub, were the blood sacrifice to ensure the safety of the rebuilding. They were a spiritual insurance covering against the walls toppling over again.

Time went by — hundreds of years — and Jericho flourished. It was conquered by Alexander the Great who made it his private estate. It became famous from one end of the ancient world to the other for the fragrance of its gardens. Its persimmon groves were said to have a perfume that 'drove men wild'. This is not the modern

orange-hued fruit but *commiphora gileadensis*, a plant that, after an absence of 1500 years from Jericho, is now being grown there again.[25] Because of its reputation, Cleopatra of Egypt — obviously keen to have the sort of power that stripped men of their rational senses — persuaded her lover Mark Antony to give her Jericho as a gift. That happened about thirty years before Jesus was born.

Herod the Great — the same Herod who ordered the massacre of the infant boys of Bethlehem — leased Jericho from Cleopatra at, reportedly, an exorbitant sum. The gardens of the winter palace he built there have only recently been uncovered by archaeologists.

These background historical details have been woven into the narrative about Zacchaeus, the tax-collector of Jericho. I believe that, in going to Jericho, Jesus acted in exactly the same way as He did

25.
As its name suggests, *commiphora gileadensis* may be the biblical 'Balm of Gilead'. It has, according to reports, a minty eucalyptus aroma. Fashions change, even in the world of perfumes. See: haaretz.com/.premium-recreating-an-ancient-israelite-perfume-1.5247057.

at Sychar, at Bethany, at Emmaus, at Gadara — He chose particular people who could represent the history of the locality. His healings therefore encompassed not just the person but the land about them with all its troubled past. He was not only healing hearts and homes but history as well.

So, because of Jericho's backstory, that always meant there would have to be two sons of Jericho to represent the city and receive mending, repairing, restoring, curing on its behalf. As Jesus left Jericho, He cured Bartimaeus and, as He then entered Jericho, He met up with Zacchaeus. This description of leaving-and-then-entering was, for a long time, seen as an error in the timing of the narration. However, it has been realised that it has geographical significance, indicating the local knowledge of the writer. Jericho had an 'old city' and a 'new city' — and Jesus was leaving one part and going on to the next.

Dictionaries variously give the meaning of Bartimaeus as *son of the unclean one* (from the Hebrew 'tame', *unclean*) or *son of honour, one who is highly prized* (from Greek 'timé', *value* or *honour*) as is found in the name Timothy. Nevertheless, I believe there was an understanding that 'timé' was connected to 'thema', for *foundation, that which is appointed or laid down or established*, thus *justice, law* or *custom*. From an etymological point of view, there is no connection. However from a poetic or popularist perspective, both this healing by Jesus and the final blessing of Paul to Timothy are suggestive of a link. In his last letter, Paul took the opportunity to bless his son in the faith, doing so in the ancient fashion of prophetically speaking into his name:

> God's *firm foundation* stands, bearing this seal: 'The Lord knows those who are His,' and, 'Let everyone who names the name of the Lord depart from iniquity.' Now in a great house there are not only vessels of gold and silver but also of wood and clay, some for *honourable* use, some for *dishonourable*. So flee youthful passions and pursue *righteousness*, faith, love, and peace, along with those who call on the Lord from a pure heart.
>
> 2 Timothy 2:19–21 ESV

The name Timothy is nuanced by those words in emphasis. So too is Bartimaeus.

Zacchaeus, on the other hand, means *man*, with the sense of a memorial. His name is a reminder. Like Segub, the son whose life was given for the gates of Jericho and whose name means *to be set on high*, Zacchaeus was associated with the gates through his position as tax-collector and he was 'set on high' through his efforts to see Jesus.

26.
See Anne Hamilton, *Dealing with Kronos: Spirit of Abuse and Time*, Armour Books 2022, for more details on the connection between covenantal crossings and Time, and water parting and Time.

27.
Like the land the Israelites were coming from when they crossed the Jordan, Eden was in the *east*. Yet *east* can also mean *before time* or *prior time*.

Bartimaeus on the other hand is a reminder of Abarim, *son for the foundation*, whose name reflects the mountain range where Moses died after climbing the peak of Nebo to view the Promised Land. Shortly afterwards, Joshua and the Israelites crossed from the eastern bank of the Jordan across to the plains of Jericho. When they came to the Jordan, it was at flood stage — swollen with ice-thaw from the north. Yet as the feet of the priests touched the water, the river backed up all the way to a locality named Adam allowing the people to cross with ease.

Like the parting of the Sea as the people left Egypt, it was a miracle symbolising the rollback of Time.[26] The Jordan crossing was specific in imaging a time that went back to 'Adam' — back to the Garden of Eden,[27] into the Land of Promise.

But that second chance went badly, just as the first one did. Jesus' actions signify yet another chance at return. Back in Eden, Adam, *man*, hid in the middle tree of the Garden after disobeying God. Most likely, it was a fig tree.[28] From there Adam watched for the coming of God as He walked through the Garden.

Zacchaeus, *man*, climbed a sycamore fig tree in Jericho, watching for God in the person of Jesus as He walked through the city of fragrant gardens.

Adam was exiled beyond the gates of Eden, but Zacchaeus is brought back from exile at the gate. The story of Zacchaeus entwines two healings — Adam's exile and Segub's sacrifice — in an extraordinarily marvellous way.

28.
Jeremy Chance Springfield at randomgroovybiblefacts.com/up-a-tree.html points out that, in the Hebrew, Adam and Eve hid in a tree, indicating they climbed it. The tree was in the middle of Eden, just as the Tree of the Knowledge of Good and Evil was, suggesting that they climbed the same tree as they'd eaten fruit from. It's likely that their fig leaves came from the same tree, indicating that its genus was most likely a variety of fig.

The righteous shall flourish like a palm tree.

Psalm 92:12 NKJV

Discussion Questions:

(1) The differences between the healing of Bartimaeus and the healing of Zacchaeus are profound. What does this tell us about asking Jesus for healing for ourselves or for others?

(2) Bartimaeus and Zacchaeus were both representatives of the history of the land and their healing was intimately entwined with it. How does this apply to your own life or impact it?

(3) Paul wrote in 2 Corinthians 2:16 BSB that we ourselves are a perfume to both believers and unbelievers alike: *'To the one, we are an odour of death and demise; to the other, a fragrance that brings life. And who is qualified for such a task?'* He rightly questions our qualifications. So how do we become qualified for such a task?

Prayer

Father of lights, who walked in Eden and talked to the man and the woman in the cool of the day, You call out to me as You did to them. You invite me into the fragrance and refreshment of Your presence. You summon me to Your banqueting table, to sit under Your songs of favour and joy.

Yet, for so many reasons — no, excuses — I am slow to accept. I waver between reluctance and enthusiasm.

Father of wisdom, help me to watch for Your coming, to watch with You in the dawnlight of Your presence. In Your grace upon grace, build in me day by day, not a knowledge of good and evil, but of You and of Your heart for this world You have made.

Father of ages, who walked in the garden of the east, in the time before time, tabernacle with me in the present, in the eternal now of Immanuel, *God with us*. Bring me into Your timeless Presence. Clothe me in Your light, armour in Your kiss, wrap me in Your prayer mantle, enfold me in Your fierce and gentle love. And cause me to turn to You and embody Your mercy, truth, justice and peace to the world. Make me a channel of Your blessing to everyone I meet. May I always see them through Your eyes.

In the name of Jesus of Nazareth. Amen.

Joppa

Jonah ran from the Lord.
He went to the seaport of Joppa and found a ship.

Jonah 1:3 CEV

Acts 9:43 NIV

Peter stayed in Joppa for some time
with a tanner named Simon.

Elijah's Mantle

A narrative retelling of the healing of the Elijah legacy from the perspective of a worker in leather-goods from the seaport of Joppa.

All week long, simple scratchings appeared in the sand between the market and the tavern, more and more of them, all the same. All week long, the drawings advanced down the main western road, as if they were on a slow, patient march to the sea.

Fish, they were. Two rough curved arcs, intersecting to represent a fish.

At first, I thought they might be almonds or eyes. That was a symbol easy to decode. I'd scrawled an almond or two back in my childhood, back in my days of dreaming. It was a symbol as old as the prophet Jeremiah who saw *shaqed*, AN ALMOND BRANCH, just awakening into flower at the beginning of spring. God commended him and said He was WATCHING, *shaqad*, over His Word.

'Wake up! Wake up and watch out!' That's what the almond shape said to me. I wondered if a school of the prophets had sprung up somewhere along the coastline. Was this their subtle way of summoning those God had called to join their company? If I'd been a few decades younger, I'd have sought them out under whatever green tree they used as a gathering place.

A few days later, by the time the drawings had made it as far as the purple-seller's house, I realised my mistake. I saw one with a kneeling figure inside and thought, 'Aha! Jonah praying in the belly of the whale.'[1] That's when I realised the diagram was not an almond or a watching eye but a fish.

Of course, I never disturbed the pictures. Not until the day I found one outside my gate. Suddenly, inexplicably, I was uneasy. I erased it. Then, even more unsettled, I glanced around to see if anyone had noticed my action.

What if the sign had nothing to do with a prophetic school? What if it had to do with a band of insurrectionists? I tried to calm my troubled thoughts. It was doubtful rebels would be so bold. More likely, it was a prank by some of the students at that tiny Greek academy on the far side of the market. Yes, that would be it — anyone with the slightest training in geometry knew about Archimedes and the measure of the fish. 153, wasn't it? And hadn't Archimedes died while drawing geometrical figures in the sand? Clearly, now I came to consider it, this was some sort of strange memorial to the old master of mathematics and philosophy.

Having convinced myself the diagrams were completely innocuous, I was unprepared for the return of the fish the next day. This time there was one on either side of my gateway. I scuffed them both out.

And then, suspicious for reasons I couldn't even begin to express, I went searching for more. The sign of the fish didn't go past my

---

1.
Kneeling and prostration is no longer common in Jewish worship except at Yom Kippur. Tiberiu Weisz in *The Kaifeng Stone Inscriptions: The Legacy of the Jewish Community in Ancient China* records that the Talmud banned kneeling and bowing because Christians adopted this practice for prayer. He contends therefore that the habit of the Chinese Jews of bowing and prostrating themselves at every service, not just at Yom Kippur, indicates the community at Kaifeng is not a recent arrival but that the people came to China at a time when this was still normal practice in worship – possibly as long ago as the Babylonian exile.

house. They didn't stride down the last few paces to the shore. They didn't follow the bend around to the watchhouse or head down the unpaved road to the south. They led to my gate. And they stopped.

I wanted to ask Serah if she'd noticed them but it was as if a hook caught my tongue every time I decided to bring it up. She was acting oddly that week. Her disposition had sweetened so suddenly and so markedly that it birthed a writhing fear in my belly. The light in her eyes, the foam of her laughter, the buoyancy of her walk, the lilt of her singing — every sign indicated to me that she was in love.

And I was afraid. I was too old to compete with some young rival. How could I contend with some bright-faced youth with clean, unscarred hands and the fresh salt tang of the sea breezing about him? I always tried hard to scrub out the noxious fumes of the tanner's trade that seeps, ineradicable, into skin and clothes before I returned home each day. But it was an impossible task.

I knew Serah loathed the smell. That's why, as soon as I could afford to, I moved the business from our home to a site with access to the Yarkon stream. And I bought Serah the finest scents — balm from Jericho and Gilead, spikenard from the east. Still nothing really can mask the repellent smells of the tannery that cling to every part of me.

And so I was afraid that I'd return one evening from the shop or the market and she'd be gone. Without a word. Without a backward glance.

I was in the middle of selling a balteus to a legionnaire when I panicked. I hurried the transaction — unusual for me — and locked the shop as soon as I could get him out. I had tried to call Serah's face into my mind's eye, and failed. Terror gripped me. I needed to get home. I needed to memorise her face, I needed to be able to recall every line and shadow. What if she left before I could remind myself of what she looked like and hide that treasure in my heart?

There were fish on the gate as I approached. Real fish on a dangling thread. It was as if the scratchings in the sand had embodied themselves with flesh and fins and shimmering scales. And there

were voices in the house. One was Serah's. Another was deeper, a male voice.

I was torn. *Flee? Or face the fear?*

I went through the gate. And strode with false confidence into the courtyard, where once my shop had been. I recognised Serah's visitor instantly and my anxiety flipped to delight. 'Simon! Cousin Simon! Shalom!' I was so relieved I actually hugged him.

'Simon! Cousin Simon! Shalom, shalom!' Startled at my demonstrative affection, he nevertheless returned my greeting in the familiar routine we'd established over the years.

'I should have realised by those fish hanging on the gate! What brings you to Joppa?' I asked. Actually Simon was Serah's cousin, not mine, but we didn't distinguish. Of all her relations, he and Andrew were the ones I felt closest to. 'Come, come,' I urged him. 'Sit down. There's a couch over in the corner here. I've missed you the last couple of years in Jerusalem. Not like you to miss Yom Kippur three years in a row.'

'I was there.' Simon nodded as he settled on the couch. His smile was careful, almost wary. 'Andrew and I were staying with friends in Bethany.'

I motioned to Serah to join us but, with an inscrutable look, she headed for the kitchen. I turned back to her cousin. How could I make an offer, sensitive but generous, one that would not offend? 'Simon, we're family.' I lowered my voice. 'Next time, come stay with us. Please. For Serah's sake. I can afford it. The business is doing well.'

'So Serah was telling me. You have your own shop now, down by the river?'

I nodded. 'A good position. Water for the tanning. Not far from the fortress. Most of the business comes from there.'

'You sell to the Romans?'

I hesitated. Opened my mouth. Closed it again. That hook I'd felt earlier was back.

Simon's smile was disarming as he searched my face. 'I wouldn't have thought there was that much call for tanned hides. Tents, maybe. Have you branched out into leather-craft?'

I decided to risk the truth. 'You know the belt the soldiers wear? The over-the-shoulder sash? The carved and decorated ones? They're very popular with the troops. High profit margin. How else do you think I've afforded all this in such a short time?' I waved my hand at the row of orange trees in pots of marble, at the low porphyry table, at the fountain at the centre of the courtyard.

Simon stared. 'What exactly do you carve into the leather?'

I knew what he was thinking. The average balteus was adorned with symbols of gods and goddesses, titans and heroes, astrological omens and good luck symbols. The officers often had gem-studded ones filled in with gold-leaf tracery. Such belts were portable wealth. 'Simon, I know you're a broad-minded man. So... promise me you won't tell any rabbi. I don't want to get thrown out of the synagogue.'

'Don't tell me Andromeda being saved by Perseus from the sea monster? The local legend?'

I scowled at him. 'Of course not. That's blasphemy. As a matter of fact, David-and-Goliath is a very popular theme. So is Daniel-and-

the-lions.' I sighed. 'No two belts are exactly alike, of course. The deal is that the purchaser gets a very much reduced price if they sit and listen to the story behind the carving. They can ask as many questions as they like.'

Simon's mouth had dropped open. There might not have been admiration in his expression but I certainly didn't sense disapproval. I was, in fact, relieved to admit what I was doing.

'Serah's family comes from Gath-hepher in Galilee, you know,' I said. 'Jonah's hometown. And here...' I pointed towards the back wall of the house. '...on the shore right outside my home is the place where the whale got indigestion and coughed up Jonah. So, the way I figure it is I married into a family with a Jonah legacy. Wouldn't that be right, Cousin Simon – Simon son of *Jonah*?'

'And the Jonah legacy would be?'

'He was called to Nineveh, remember. That makes him not just the only prophet from Galilee but also the only one called to preach face-to-face with the Gentiles.'

'You're preaching to Gentiles?' Simon's mouth fell into a fish-like gape.

'Not exactly. I'm telling stories. And I'm sending soldiers out into the world, wearing the stories of our people. I'm teaching them the story so that when they are asked what the meaning of the balteus is, they can retell it in a foreign land.' I grinned at him. 'You know what my bestseller is?'

He shook his head in obvious disbelief.

'I make paraclete pairs. A matching set for a soldier and his paraclete. The partners like to buy one for each other. They almost always try to vie with each other to pay extra, because it's a gift to the one safeguarding them. I listen to their stories about how they saved each other in battle and risked their lives for each other, and then they listen to me. The saga of David-and-Jonathan is a natural favourite, so is Jonathan-and-his-armour-bearer.' I turned off my grin and eyed Simon seriously. 'You could give up fishing, you know, and make an absolute fortune out of leather craft.'

'I have given up fishing.'

Serah arrived with a platter of lamb wrapped in vine leaves and mint, olives, grapes, bread and oil. A curious look passed between the two of them, a look I couldn't interpret.

'And I'm no longer Simon. My name is now Peter.' He took the bread, blessed it, broke it and handed a piece to me. 'Cousin, may I tell you what I've been doing for the last three years?'

May I? What? When did rough, tough Simon the fisherman, oops, ex-fisherman, oops, ex-Simon, when did he get manners? I glanced from him to Serah and back again. 'Sure,' I said warily.

And so the afternoon passed, and the evening. Nightfall came and Serah lit the oil lamps. And still Simon spoke on and on. One story after another. I listened intently, sometimes asking a question. I'd learned in my line of work how to encourage the small detail, the seemingly inconsequential clarification that revealed the heart behind my customers' gruff exteriors so I could find the perfect faith story to inspire them.

Not that Peter needed any of the encouragement my clientele sometimes did. I let him ramble on because I saw how much pleasure

the stories gave Serah. And I peppered him with questions because, mysteriously, they seemed to give her even deeper delight. Left to myself, I would have cried, 'Enough!' after an hour, but we went on and on, story after story about Jesus of Nazareth.

I'd heard about Him, of course, and except for one thing I'd have been desperately worried the moment I realised He was the man Serah was crazywild in love with — this wonderworker of Galilee, this miracle-maker and rustic teacher with the shrewd wit and the lancing tongue who was able to spear the various species of snake in our society, all the lawyers, scribes, Pharisees and Sadducees, and pin them in their place. The one thing that reassured me was the knowledge that Jesus was dead. There had been people here in Joppa who had hoped He was the Messiah and had travelled to Jerusalem to hear Him, ready to join His cause if they were satisfied by His claims. But they came back after Passover with news of His death.

Except, according to Peter, He wasn't dead. I was briefly concerned until I learned He'd gone to heaven. It was very late when Peter finally stopped and Serah asked me what I thought.

'What do I think?' Finally it dawned on me what this meeting was all about. Serah had been afraid to tell me she'd become a follower of The Way. And so she'd asked her cousin Simon, sorry, Peter, to come and explain it to me. He'd done her a very great honour, really. If I understood correctly, he was now the leader of The Way, and yet he'd taken the time to come at her request.

'Do you believe?' Serah asked me.

I faltered. 'Ahhh... believe what?'

Peter rescued me. 'Cousin,' he said to Serah. 'I've overwhelmed him. And the resurrection of Jesus is so incredible, I'm sure he needs to consider whether I am telling the truth.' He shrugged, and his smile seemed diffident in the lamplight.

I didn't need to consider if he was speaking truth. That wasn't the issue at all. I can tell when someone is genuine and when they're

trying to frame a story to enhance their own legend. The secret of my business success is all about listening and finding the true heart of the story and the ancient echoes of faith pulsing through it. So because Peter was telling the story, I was focused on his part in it all, not on Jesus.

It was actually his second-to-last story, the one before the coming of the Holy Spirit, that had arrested me. The story of meeting a man by the Sea, of recognising Jesus and flinging on a mantle to jump overboard and meet Him, of finding bread baked on hot coals waiting on the shore, of harvesting 153 fish, of a gentle rebuff and a summons to return to an abandoned calling. The details teased at me. There was another story with mantles and bread baked on hot coals, with 153 and the appeal to return to a forsaken calling.

I could sense the prophetic weight in Peter's retelling — and not just for him, but for Serah and me. Why had Jesus three times called him 'Simon, son of Jonah' at that breakfast if his name now was Peter? It was portentous. I could feel it. But I was tired and couldn't retrieve the pattern I was seeking.

We left it at that for the evening and Serah made up a sleep-couch for him. As she lay beside me later, in the darkness, stiff and still, I whispered to her, 'I'm sorry.'

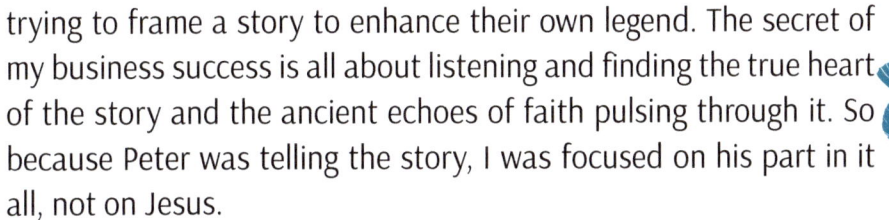

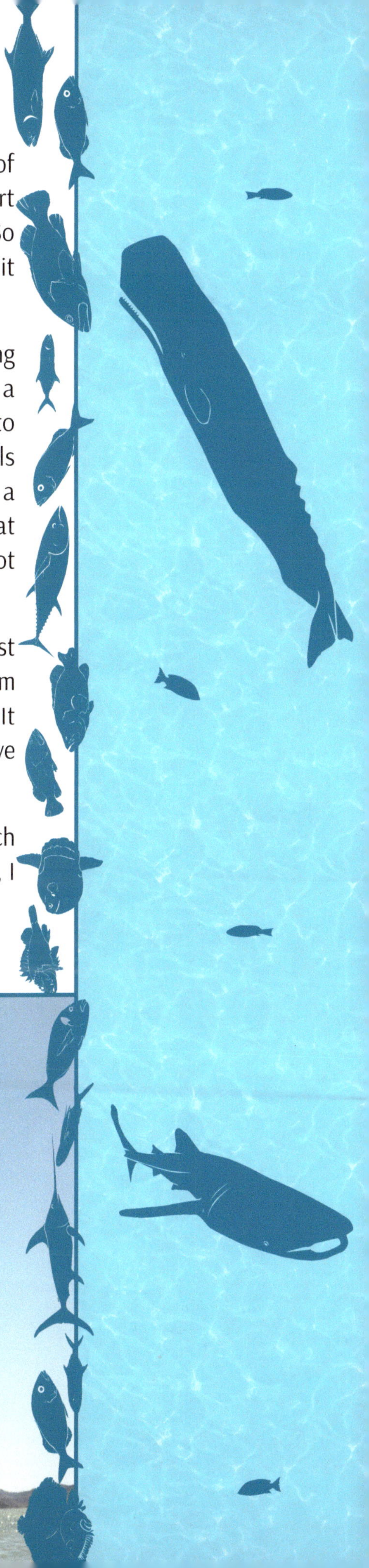

'There's no need,' she sighed, her breath a feather in the air. 'I didn't really expect you to believe.'

But you hoped. 'I wasn't apologising for not believing,' I told her. 'That is a gift of The Name, blessed be He. I cannot force it, just respond to it. I was saying sorry, Serah, because I have made you so afraid that you could not tell me this news yourself.' I inclined my head towards her. 'I would never want to make you afraid, Serah. You are the most precious thing in my life.'

'You never spend time with me.'

Her cracked voice was so soft I wasn't sure I heard right. *She wanted to be around me? What could I say to that?* 'I thought I could give you things to explain that I love you, but clearly that is a strategy that is not working particu...' I was cut off by her sudden movement and the touch of her lips on my mouth.

'You think too much,' she said.

I woke early the following morning and crept outside, padding down to the shore to watch the waves come in and greet the dawn. And, grateful beyond measure to The Name, I sang the salvation song of Jonah to welcome the day:

> I called to the Lord in my distress, and He answered me. From the depths of my watery grave I cried for help, and You heard my cry.
>
> You threw me into the deep, into the depths of the sea, and water surrounded me. All the whitecaps on Your waves have swept over me.
>
> Then I thought, 'I have been banished from Your sight. Will I ever see Your holy temple again?'
>
> Water surrounded me, threatening my life. The deep covered me completely. Seaweed was wrapped around my head.
>
> I sank to the foot of the mountains. I sank to the bottom, where bars held me forever. But You brought me back from the pit, O Lord, my God.
>
> As my life was slipping away, I remembered the Lord. My prayer came to You in Your holy temple.
>
> Those who hold on to worthless idols abandon their loyalty to You.

But I will sacrifice to You with songs of thanksgiving. I will keep my vow. Victory belongs to the Lord![2]

I hadn't known how deeply I had slipped into the pit of depression, drowning under the waves of a perpetual anxiety Serah would leave me. I'd feared her going for years and tried to hold her lightly. Instead I'd pushed her away. Whatever I eventually decided about Jesus as the Messiah, I would still have to thank Him for one thing — for Serah's love. I had never realised its deeps before, never felt secure in it.

I knelt, my robes lapped by the waves, and gave thanks to The Name, blessed be He, for the one called Jesus of Nazareth. *Was He the Messiah? If so, why hadn't He stayed after His resurrection? Why wasn't He still here?* Peter had answered that with some explanation about the Holy Spirit, but it struck me as far too convenient that an allegedly once-dead man was not around to testify to Himself.

'Simon!'

It was Peter, calling. I turned to meet him. He came down the sand, a dark silhouette with the rising sun limning his shoulders like a mantle of light and, in that moment, I remembered the old, old story with the breakfast of bread baked on hot coals, the number 153, and the call back to a vocation that had been thrown over in panic and depression. The mantle of Elijah the prophet had passed, wonder beyond wonders, to my wife's foot-in-mouth cousin from Bethsaida in Galilee.

And in that moment I also knew that, in his weakness, Peter would make the same mistakes that Elijah had.

'I came to say goodbye,' Peter said. 'And to thank you for being so understanding, for listening without resistance or anger.'

Goodbye? No. Not yet. 'You'll stay for breakfast.' I didn't ask, I made it a command. 'I still have some questions.' *What could I ask?* 'About the Holy Spirit.'

Peter was thrilled.

'Let me show you the spot Jonah was spat out by the whale.' I pointed him just a little way up the beach. 'You know what the stomach acid of fish does to skin?'

2. Jonah 2:2–9 GWT

'Turns it white.'

'You know? Of course you know. You're a fisherman.' I laughed to cover my blunder. 'Former fisherman, I mean. Now fishing for men.' I pointed to the location and adopted my most serious tone. 'You know what I find so marvellous about this story, son of Jonah? Not the whale, or the great fish, whatever it was. But the protection God arranged for Jonah. He was sent to Nineveh, *the house of the fish*, with bleached skin. The priests of Nineveh, worshippers of a fish-deity, would have taken one look and realised the significance of his appearance. Instead of taking a sword to him the moment he opened his mouth and prophesied destruction for them all, they'd have been completely awed by a message that had come from the belly of a fish in the heart of the sea.'

'Jesus spoke of His dying and rising as the sign of the prophet Jonah.'

'Did He?' I slotted that small detail into my net of facts about Elijah's mantle and nodded. I turned for home and kept Peter talking. He told me of a time when Jesus had sent Him to catch a fish with a shekel in its mouth in order to pay the Temple tax.[3] That too, we surmised together was a sign of the prophet Jonah — the Temple shekel had an image of Herakles Melqart on it, *Hercules of the city of the underworld.* As Jonah was three days in the underworld, in a pit inside a fish, in an unearthly grave, so Jesus was three days in the bowels of Death.

3. Matthew 17:27

Over breakfast, we chatted more. I desisted from leaving for the tannery, in case Peter took the opportunity to go. A compulsion, even stronger than the one I'd had to memorise Serah's face, was upon me. I had to keep Peter in the house. It was imperative.

We rambled through more stories, started to repeat ourselves, found half the morning was gone, considered broaching a jar of wine. I managed to persuade him to rest a little up on the roof overlooking the atrium, while the midday meal was prepared. He allowed himself to be convinced because he wanted to spend time praying.

Serah eyed me, askance, when I came back down and whispered to her, 'We have to delay his leaving as long as possible.'

'Why?' she asked, even as she nodded. 'What are you up to, Simon?'

'Can't you see the Elijah mantle on him? Can't you see the protection and the danger?'

She stared at me, not as if I'd taken leave of my senses, but as if appraising a curiosity. 'Elijah? What do you mean "Elijah"? You've been talking about nothing but Jonah with him. I thought you were trying to hint that he had Jonah's legacy, Jonah's mantle, Jonah's birthright upon him.'

'Yes. Same thing, my sweet. Same thing.' I was about to explain when I heard Peter stumbling around on the roof. Grabbing a jug of water, I darted away and hurried up the steps where I found him, swaying and looking dazed. 'Come, come.' I led him to a couch. 'Sit. You look unsteady.'

'Just a dream,' he said. 'A vision. I'm not sure what to make of it. It happened three times.'

Three times? Has he been on the roof long enough for that? I shrugged. *What is time when you are gazing into eternity?*

'It was a sheet, a sail, a cloth full of unclean animals. It unfurled itself and descended from heaven. Then there was a Voice that said, "Arise, Peter, kill and eat!" I protested this but the Voice said I was not to call unclean...'[4]

There was a clanging at the gateway and a yell. 'Is this the house of Simon the tanner?'

'...what God has called clean. I have no idea what this means.' Peter blinked, looking slightly less confused. 'I need to think and meditate on it.'

The gate rattled again. 'I'll get it,' I called to Serah, nodding apologetically at Peter. I dashed back down the stairs and into the courtyard. Through the iron bars at the gate, I could see a staff officer from one of the legions. *Italian regiment*, I thought, *if I'm not mistaken.* A chariot was behind him and he was accompanied by two stout and sturdy servants with a wagon. There weren't any balteus commissions outstanding, and definitely not for anyone in the Italian regiment. They were stationed at Caesarea Maritima, a full day's march up the coast. I wondered why they were here.

'Is Simon also known as Peter staying here?' the staff officer asked.[5]

And in that instant I knew what it was about. Jonah's unfinished mission to the Gentiles.

Peter had come down from the roof and walked up behind me. 'I'm the man you're looking for,' he said. 'Why are you here?'

The staff officer cleared his throat. 'Cornelius, a centurion and an upright and God-fearing man who is respected by the whole Jewish nation, was instructed by a holy angel to send for you to come to his home to hear what you have to say.'[6]

Peter looked at me.

'Welcome them in,' I said to him. 'You won't make it to Caesarea today.'

---

4. Acts 10:13 NASB

5. Acts 10:18

6. Acts 10:22 ISV

He looked rather shell-shocked at the prospect, but I left him to talk to the Romans while I went to warn Serah to rustle up more food. She grabbed my sleeve as I went back out to rescue Peter. It would be easy enough. I was a balteus-maker and story-teller.

'You are not leaving me behind,' Serah stated. 'I am going with you to Caesarea.'

'It's dangerous,' I protested. 'But...' I immediately relented, '...on an assignment for The Name, it should be safe enough. And you're right, I may need your support when Peter speaks before he thinks, and so offends this centurion Cornelius.'

Serah glared. 'Why have you never told me you are a seer?'

'What? Me? Don't be ridiculous!' I dashed away. I did a lot of dashing that day.

By the evening, I had made the acquaintance of half the followers of The Way in Joppa, heard about Peter's raising of a local seamstress Dorcas, fended off a dozen attempts to nudge Serah and me out of the expedition to Caesarea, learned the group were also called Christians and that they were the ones who'd scrawled the fish symbol in the sand, and discovered the staff officer's secret penchant for quoting

extensive passages from the books of Enoch and Daniel. He was so devout that, given half a chance, he'd have made theological mincemeat out of every student of prophecy in the room. So I encouraged Peter to tell stories and talk about the resurrection late into the evening.

We set out for Caesarea the following morning. The wagon and the chariot were a thoughtful gesture as it turned out, making it an easy journey.

Serah sat next to me, her head on my shoulder, insisting on a story. 'You tell Roman soldiers epic tales of faith,' she whispered with a scowl. 'But not me. I want the story of Elijah's mantle and why it's here with us in this cart.'

'You don't need to be educated,' I whispered back. 'You're not ignorant. You are aglow with faith.'

'Elijah's mantle.' Her voice was stern.

No, not a story. She only wanted that because I'd given it to others. *What does she really want?* I thought back to all the stories Peter had told, trying to remember the ones where she'd leaned in closer. *I think...* Yes, Serah had accused me of thinking too much, but still I thought. *I think it was the one about the two women, one in the kitchen, one at the rabbi's feet. Aha... she wanted to learn.* I cast my mind back decades, to my childhood when I'd sat at an old rabbi's feet learning the stories I was passing on. I adopted his quiet, studious tone. 'Let me first begin with some questions. Who inherited Elijah's mantle?'

She answered without hesitation. 'Elisha.'

'See, your education shows already. Who inherited Elijah's mantle from Elisha?'

There was a long pause as Serah looked at me sideways. 'One of the sons of the prophets.'

'Which one?'

A longer pause. 'Jonah?' she asked doubtfully.

I nodded. She looked dubious, but I pressed on. 'Yes, Jonah. He was the young prophet sent by Elisha to anoint the army commander Jehu as king of Israel.'

'We're going to see an army commander right now,' Serah pointed out.

'I can't see Peter doing any anointing so we'll have to see how that works out in a different way.' I winked at her. 'Remember when Elijah was running from Jezebel after the great confrontation at Mount Carmel? What happened when he got to Beersheba?'

'He went out into the desert, sat under a broom tree and complained he wanted to die. Then he went to sleep and woke up to a breakfast of…' She stopped, hesitated. I could almost see her thoughts whirring. '…bread baked on hot coals by an angel. Just like the breakfast for Peter by the lake.'

'Elijah was supposed to go back, just as Peter was called to go back. But when Elijah didn't, what did God ask him to do?'

'Anoint Elisha to succeed him, anoint Jehu king of Israel, anoint Hazael king of Aram.'

'My clever wife. You want to be a student, don't you? When you should be a teacher.'

Her sudden smile was radiant. 'But you said Jonah anointed Jehu.'

'Indeed. That means neither Elijah nor Elisha did. It was over twenty years before Jehu was anointed, twenty years when Ahab and his sons ruled, worshipping idols and dominated by Jezebel. Hard question: who anointed Hazael?'

It was a long time before the answer came. 'No one.' Serah paused. 'Elisha told him he would be king but did not anoint him.'

'Correct. Neither Elijah nor Elisha anointed the Gentile; nor gave instructions to one of their protégés for it to happen.' I stroked her veil. 'So what does this tell us about the mantle that passed from Elijah to Elisha to Jonah?'

Serah sucked in a deep breath. 'Extreme reluctance to fulfil any mission concerning Gentiles.' Her gaze slanted towards Peter. 'This is trouble. But how did he get the mantle?'

"Come and have breakfast."
John 21:12 NIV

'Weren't you listening to those stories yesterday? John the Baptist was given the Elijah mantle, Jesus took it on after John died and He gave it to your cousin at the breakfast by the lake. Bread baked on hot coals and all that. 153 fish and all that. Remember the very last story of Elijah and the 153 troops sent to summon him to appear before the king? That's why Jesus kept stressing "Simon, son of *Jonah*," and referring to his clothing. It's because the Elijah mantle passed to Jonah, making them the same mantle.'

'We need to pray, Simon.'

I sighed heavily. 'What we really need is a paraclete, my love. A companion to stand back-to-back with us in this centuries-old battle. I now know why those Romans feel so secure when they have someone loyal to depend on.'

My wife looked at me as if I'd had some profound, divine inspiration. 'Did Peter tell you about what Jesus calls the Holy Spirit or did you just come up with that revelation yourself?'

I frowned at her. 'What revelation?'

'Jesus calls the Holy Spirit "the Paraclete". Actually, the "*other* Paraclete."'

I felt a seismic shift in my soul. 'You pray,' I said to Serah. 'I'll meditate on paracletes.' And so I did, all the way to Caesarea. By the time we got there, I had made the decision to ask Jesus and the Holy Spirit to be my paracletes the first time the opportunity presented itself. There was, no doubt, a ceremony to go with such a momentous surrender.

Well, we got to Caesarea and it didn't take more than three sentences before Peter brought out the knife of offence.

Cornelius met us at the gate of his house with a prostrate bow. The emperor himself couldn't have got a more deferential welcome. 'Stand up!' Peter said. 'I'm only a man.'[7]

So far, so good. Then things went downhill: 'You understand how wrong it is for a Jew to associate or visit with unbelievers. But God has shown me that I should stop calling anyone common or unclean, and that is why I didn't hesitate when I was sent for. Now may I ask why you sent for me?'[8]

Cornelius was courtesy itself. He explained the vision and the instructions he'd received from the angel.

I could see Serah's lips moving in silent prayer.

7.
Acts 10:26 NIV

8.
Acts 10:28–29 NIV

"I will ask the Father, and He will give you another advocate to help you and be with you forever - the Spirit of truth."

John 14:16-17 NIV

Peter launched away with an announcement about God not showing partiality which I found difficult to assess. Maybe it was a backhanded accusation of God in the best tradition of Jonah complaining about God's mercy to pagans, or maybe it was a commendation of God's lack of prejudice when it came to the racial makeup of devout believers. Fortunately, Peter jettisoned that quicksand statement and just began to proclaim Jesus.

'Paraclete,' I said under my breath. 'I prostrate my soul. We need You. *Now*. Hurry.'

And, with a frisson of light that set my whole body tingling, another Presence entered the room. It swept through like a stormwind off the sea, it flickered with spear-heads of flame and spoke with the sound of many waters. The anointing had come — in light and fire. I could see the oil pouring from the highest heaven on the head of Cornelius and his family.

The centurion seemed suddenly, to me, cloaked in the lustrous green leaves of a fruit tree. He called to his staff officer, and his servants began shouting in unison. I didn't know the language they were speaking but I knew they were praising God.

'Well done, Paraclete!' I cried, raising jubilant balled fists. The entire room turned to stare at me. I didn't recognise the tongue I'd spoken, but I knew that they all knew exactly what I said.

I must be wrong. There's no ceremony at all. Just the heart-lifting wonder of knowing the assignment given to Jonah so long ago had been brought to fruition, and that finally the bearer of Elijah's mantle had anointed the Gentiles.

I laughed. I clapped my hands, then threw my arms around Serah, my everyday paraclete. *How have I never realised that before?*

And I also realised as I looked at Peter, standing there astonished, that one day he would try to walk this moment back. But it would be too late. The incoming of the Gentiles, long-delayed by men, long-awaited by God, had finally begun.

Monsters from the Deep

The story of Jonah and his journey in the belly of the whale is too much for some people to swallow. It is simply too great a strain on their credulity.

Back in Peter's day, however, the people of Joppa wouldn't have had any problem at all. They knew gigantic wild creatures rode the sea currents and glided through the crushing darkness of the ocean floor. Such enormous monsters were, they knew first-hand, subject to the bidding of divine beings and were ready to retaliate on their behalf against humans who offended them. If there was any strangeness in Jonah's story, it was that the God of the Hebrews was merciful not vengeful.

Contrast Jonah's story with that of Andromeda. In classical mythology, Andromeda's mother, queen of Aethiopia, unwisely boasts of her own beauty, saying it surpassed that of the nymphs of the sea. These nymphs were attendants of Poseidon and, insulted, he sent a sea monster to ravage the coasts. In an attempt to appease the monster, Andromeda was chained to a rock as an offering where she was rescued by the hero Perseus.

In a first century retelling by Conon, the sacrificial rock on the coasts of Aethiopia was located at Joppa. Andromeda's father was Cepheus, so very reminiscent of the Hebrew version of Peter — Cephas, *rock*. In fact, Cephas is more accurately *cornerstone* or *sacrificial rock*, thus evoking a link with the legend of Joppa circulating in his own era.

Notice some similarities and differences:

- Andromeda was sacrificed by the people of Joppa to placate a sea monster stirred up by Poseidon to bring about vengeance.
- Jonah was sacrificed by the sailors of Joppa to placate the sea that was stirred up by Yahweh to bring about repentance.

The great monstrous fish that seemed like an agent of vengeance was, in fact, a messenger of mercy. The monster sent by Poseidon was brutal, violent, savage, voracious. The whale — or, more accurately, the 'great fish' since the Hebrew does not actually mention whale — may well have been the same but, surrendered to the will of God, it proved to be a severe mercy in Jonah's life.

Jonah didn't just preach to the people of Nineveh. His story — through its startling contrast with the local tale of Andromeda — was a proclamation to the people of Joppa about the nature of the Most High God. It's no coincidence that the message at Nineveh is the message at Joppa: no matter how deeply you've offended the Lord of heaven, He is willing to be merciful if you turn back to Him. And if you do, He will tame the monsters that would otherwise destroy you.

Notes

The story of Elijah makes it clear that Elisha received his mantle as well as a double portion of his spirit. It seems possible that Elisha died without passing that mantle on. However, Jewish tradition hints that this is not the case. It identifies by name the young man tasked by Elisha with going to the frontier fortress where Jehu was stationed and anointing him king. In 2 Kings 9, Elisha simply summons an anonymous member of the company of prophets, 'one of the sons of the prophets', and tells him to go to Ramoth Gilead, take Jehu aside privately, anoint him and then run for it as fast as he can.

> Elisha the prophet called one of the sons of the prophets and said to him, 'Tie up your garments, and take this flask of oil in your hand, and go to Ramoth-gilead. And when you arrive, look there for Jehu the son of Jehoshaphat, son of Nimshi. And go in and have him rise from among his fellows, and lead him to an inner chamber. Then take the flask of oil and pour it on his head and say, "Thus says the Lord, I anoint you king over Israel." Then open the door and flee; do not linger.'
>
> 2 Kings 9:1–3 ESV

Although Scripture does not name this young man in this record, there is a widespread Jewish belief that he was Jonah — in his younger days, before God called him to preach to the people of Nineveh. If it is correct that this is indeed the case, and I believe it is, then Elijah's mantle which passed to Elisha would then have passed to his disciple, Jonah.

Now most of the time, if ever a question arises about a prophet disobeying God, the majority of us would automatically think of Jonah. Elijah and Elisha, for whatever mysterious reason, are heroes with haloes. Yet a close examination of their stories highlights some tragic character flaws. If Jonah was mentored by Elisha, then he had some excellent role models when it came to defiance of God.

Elijah was authorised by God to anoint two kings, but he never did so. Elisha clearly knew that Elijah had not executed these assignments, and that the delay had resulted in many calamities.

Worse than simply failing to seek out Jehu, it's clear that Elijah had actually met up with him at least once. This becomes evident when Jehu mentions he was present with Ahab as a dire prophecy was being delivered concerning the murder of Naboth. But that word of divine retribution was declared by Elijah — making it clear that he'd encountered Jehu but had let the moment pass.

Elisha too let the moment pass. For another twelve years. It's unclear how long it took before Jehu was anointed after God commissioned Elijah to do so at Mount Horeb, but it was sometime between 21 and 37 years! Decades full of unnecessary tragedy. Elijah simply defied God outright, and Elisha waited a very long time before passing the authority to one of his disciples — as least in the case of Jehu.

When it came to Hazael, both Elijah and Elisha baulked. Just as Elijah missed a chance when meeting with Jehu, Elisha missed a chance when meeting with Hazael. Elisha revealed Hazael would be king but did not anoint him.

Notice the pattern of reluctance across the three prophets, Elijah, Elisha and Jonah. It's not simply about the Gentiles, though that clearly brings out even more pronounced insubordination. They just did not approve God's choice, so they delayed obeying — and in the process created heartbreak for many people.

Now the reason I think the Jewish tradition about Jonah being the unidentified young prophet is correct is because Jesus implies it is so. The whole of the last scene in John's gospel is charged with allusions to Elijah, though he is never mentioned directly. There are only two breakfasts cooked by a divine personage in Scripture and both consist of bread baked on coals. Both are made for someone running away from his calling. The emphasis on clothing, on passing on a charge, on 153 — which also has a nuance of inheritance — and even that final protest that Jesus never said John was not going to die (so reminiscent of Elijah taken up to heaven) reinforces this. In addition, the final chapter is constructed as a mirror reflection of the first chapter where John the Baptist denies he is the Elijah-who-is-to-come, although we know from the testimony of Jesus that he is.

Echoes of Elijah underpin the last scene and, throughout it, John very subtly made the point that, despite what people might think, he was not given the mantle of Elijah the prophet. That honour went to Peter who is continually and very peculiarly addressed by Jesus as 'Simon, son of Jonah.' Yet if the mantle of Elijah was passed through Elisha to Jonah, this is no oddity at all.

For the healing of history to occur, the location is important. The critical moment of choice in Jonah's life, the natural point of no return — barring, of course, the intervention of God — was at the harbour of Joppa where he took ship for Tarshish at the edge of the known world. It is thought that Tarshish was located near the modern city of Cadiz. It would therefore have been the Phoenician port of Gades, with a temple to Melqart-Moloch-Kronos.[3] Kronos, the leader of the titans in Greek mythology, was renowned for swallowing his children and later being forced to disgorge them. Like the great fish who swallowed Jonah and was later forced to spew him out.

I have to wonder what those Phoenician sailors did when they finally returned from Tarshish to Joppa and heard what happened to the Hebrew they'd thrown overboard. Did they see that Yahweh, the Lord of Lords and Most High God, was having a playful poke at the violent deity they worshipped?

The link between Jonah and Melqart, who was depicted on the Temple shekel, was brought to the fore by Jesus when He instructed Peter to go fishing and bring back a fish that had a shekel in its mouth to pay the tax. This is a reversal of the Jonah motif because, rather than Jonah being in the fish, it is now Melqart, god of the underworld, trapped by the fish.

The expulsion of the money-lenders from the Temple is symbolic of the driving out of Herakles-Melqart, imaged on their coins. Furthermore this scene is paralleled, in John's very stylised mirror-reflective design, by the ejection of Death from the tomb of Jesus.

The 'death of Death' and resurrection symbolism is enhanced by the number 153.

> So Simon Peter went aboard and dragged the net ashore. It was full of large fish, 153, but even with so many, the net was not torn.
>
> John 21:11 BSB

It seems such an inconsequential detail, but there is so much packed into that brief reference. 153 was part of a well-known geometrical theorem which had been around for centuries prior to the era of Jesus. Because of its shape, it was called 'the measure of the fish'.[4] In our century, we've

3.
This is said to be at the site of what is now San Sebastián castle.

4.
Archimedes had discovered it in the ratio of the chord to the radius of intersecting circles that pass through each other's centres and form a fish-like overlap.

5.
The skeleton of 153 is 1 — 5 — 3.
A trinity function applied to the skeleton is the same as cubing. 1^3 — 5^3 — 3^3.
Expanding this is 1x1x1 — 5x5x5 — 3x3x3.
Which is 1 — 125 — 27.
Add these together and the total is 153.

7.
Galatians 2:12

6.
See, for more details on 153 as a motif of inheritance the appendices in *Dealing with Belial: Spirit of Armies and Abuse*, Armour Books 2022.

Greg Stigter has also pointed out to me that, in Mark's gospel, there were 153 instances of the use of the historic present tense. Hardly coincidental!

Joppa itself, as indicated in the nineteenth century book, *Picturesque Palestine, Sinai and Egypt, volume 3*, has a curious 153 inbuilt into the landscape as this segment of text shows: 'Jaffa, or rather Yâfa, is one of the oldest seaports in the world, and its name has been preserved almost unchanged from the earliest times… *Yapho*, "the beautiful"… No change has been made in the site of the city: the Jaffa of the present century stands on the accumulated ruins of former cities, on a rounded hill, the summit of which is one hundred and fifty-three feet above the level of the sea… Just in front of the town there is a semicircular belt of rocks, some of which rise high out of the water, while others are only indicated by the surf which dashes over them. These rocks (to one of which, according to Pliny, Andromeda was chained) form a large but shallow harbour, which can only be entered by small boats.' Joppa is currently called Yafo. The city of Tel Aviv has developed around it.

I should also point out that, because I like to use the kind of numerical literary style found in the Scriptures—a very basic level, I admit—this section entitled 'NOTES' is 1530 words long.

"Come, follow Me," Jesus said, "and I will make you fishers of men."

Matthew 4:19, Mark 1:17 NIV

largely discarded geometry as an important component of a good education, but in classical times it was considered essential.

Now 153 has a peculiar property: it is the first number that can be reconstructed from its own skeleton by using a trinity function. In reconstituting itself, it's the ideal number to symbolise resurrection.[5] In addition, it is a number associated with the children of God.[6] It is integral to the identification of God's family and to the process of inheritance. It should therefore not be surprising to find it mentioned in a story about the handing on of Elijah's legacy.

153, after all, is hidden in the story of Elijah. In the very last incident before his disappearance to heaven, three troops of fifty men, along with their commanding officers, are sent by Ahab's son, Ahaziah, to bring Elijah to him. Two of the three squadrons are destroyed by fire from heaven. The 153rd man, the captain of the third troop, pleads with Elijah to hold off on calling down more divine retribution.

All these small details show that Jesus, on the shores by the Sea of Galilee, was setting up a long-term strategy for the healing of history that went back through Jonah to Elijah. No question that, had Peter refused to go with the men Cornelius sent to Joppa, the Holy Spirit would have found another way.

There would be no more waiting decades like Jehu and Hazael did. But even in this story we see the lengths to which the Holy Spirit had to go to overcome Peter's reluctance — not just a triple vision but actually intervening to impart the anointing Himself. Clearly that reluctance was never fully overcome because we also see, some years later, that Paul had to confront Peter when he stopped eating with the Gentiles after some men came from James in Jerusalem.[7]

This is the strongest possible lesson to us not to grieve the Holy Spirit by unconscionable delay.

Discussion Questions:

(1) After Elijah's great victory on Mount Carmel, he is threatened by Jezebel and never fully recovers. Yet rather than follow God's instructions to anoint Jehu — which would have meant the end of her reign — he does nothing. Why do you think he chooses to live in fear of a woman rather than fear of God?

(2) Are we slow to obey God because we've been trained that way? Or is there some other reason?

(3) Oftentimes leaders won't appoint someone they know has a divine calling upon their life because they assess that they're 'not ready'. Yet if the person were totally ready they would be far less likely to rely on God than if they know they're not ready. What are the issues for leaders who resist making the appointments God has asked of them?

 Prayer

Loving Father,

I think of all the wasted time. Generations of it. People who were called and who waited, year upon year, for the anointing that came so late. That, sometimes, never came.

I think of the hope deferred that makes the heart sick — for surely, Lord, You place a calling in the heart and train Your chosen ones for their vocation. One that seems to recede further with every passing year.

I think of Your Holy Spirit grieved by those who consider themselves better judges than You of the type of person You should call. Better judges of others' readiness for the role. Better judges of character. Better judges of the position others should be allotted in Your kingdom.

Loving Father,

I ask You to redeem the time wasted. I ask You to heal the hearts sick from depression because hope has been too long deferred. I ask You to convict those who see themselves as judges more capable than You. I ask for the intervention of Your Holy Spirit so that any healing of history You want me to participate in is not delayed. I ask You to rebuke Time itself and return to me the years the locusts have eaten so that, while it is late for any anointing, it is not too late. Grant to me, Lord, all that is needed to complete Your will for me and for my family, community and nation. Give me the courage to acknowledge Your will as good and perfect. Give me the courage to obey Your will as good and perfect. Give me the courage to fulfil Your will as good and perfect.

I ask this in the name of Jesus, the master-strategist of heaven who appoints the redeeming of time, the mending of the world and the healing of history.

Amen.

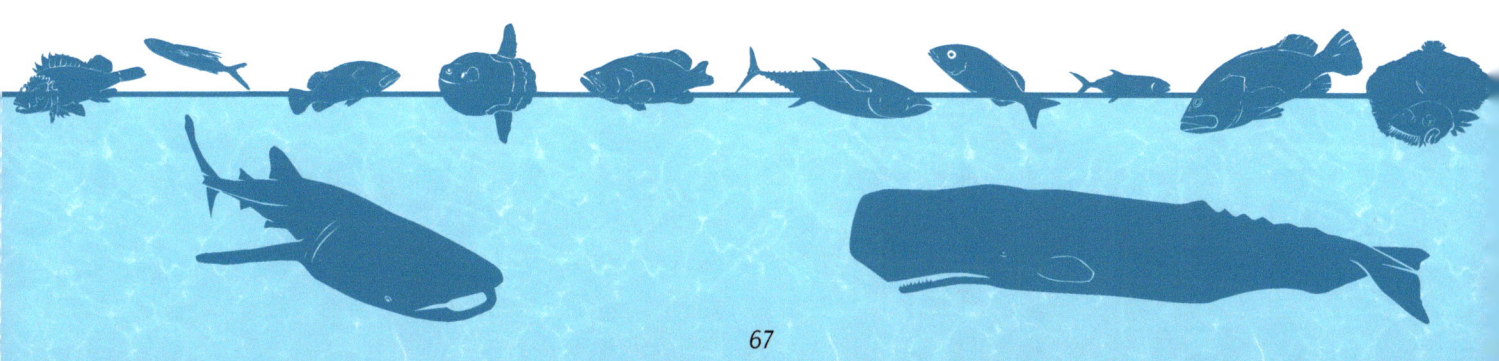

Acknowledgments & Attributions

Photo and Art Credits

Front cover and page 4 – FOTO4440/ Depositphotos | Description: Whale tail fluke;
Racim Amr/ Unsplash | Description: Body of water under cloudy sky during daytime

Back cover – x-reflexnaja/ iStock | Description: Asian fisherman throwing fishing net during twilight on wooden boat at the lake.

Page 5 – David Clode/ Unsplash | Description: green and yellow rope on gray metal fence

Page 7 – slavapolo/ Depositphotos | Description: Oasis in Judean Desert at Wadi Qelt near Jericho

Page 8 – YAYImages/ Depositphotos | Description: Excavations near Jericho city of ancient palace

Page 10 – DesignPicsInc/ Depositphotos | Description: Pharisees; Kathryn Farley/ Getty Images: Canaanite gate closeup, Jericho

Page 11 – LUMO–The Gospels for the visual age/ Lightstock | Description: Judas agrees to betray Jesus

Page 12 – spanic/ Getty Images | Description: Roman soldiers preparing to fight

Page 13 – Gaby Yerden/ Unsplash | Description: Fig thyme shrub cocktail

Page 14 – DesignPicsInc/ Depositphotos | Description: Jesus leads three disciples up a hill

Page 15 – majaFOTO/ Depositphotos | Description: Ancient sycamore tree in Jericho

Page 17 – ValenZi/ iStock | Description: Ficus sycomorus, sycamore figs, fig-mulberry, naturalised species in Israel

Page 18 – Vicky Ng/Unsplash | Description: n/a

Page 20 – LUMO–The Gospels for the visual age/ Lightstock | Description: Zacchaeus The Tax Collector

Page 21 – LUMO–The Gospels for the visual age/ Lightstock | Description: Zacchaeus The Tax Collector

Page 23 – LUMO–The Gospels for the visual age/ Lightstock | Description: Zacchaeus The Tax Collector

Page 26 – ratpack2/Depositphotos | Description: Angel resting on a pillar

Page 27 – Public domain/ University of Amsterdam | Description: Balsamodendron_ehrenbergianum00

Page 30 – eunikas/ Depositphotos | Description: Historic and modern city of Jericho

Page 31 – marzolino/ Depositphotos | Description: Ficus sycomorus

Page 32 – anke/ canstockphoto | Description: Jesus healing the lame man

Page 35 – Danita Delimont/ Alamy | Description: Israel, Joppa, City street

Page 36 – Forgiven Photography/ Lightstock | Description: Jesus walking on a beach

Page 37 – Beckon Creative | Description: ichthus in sand

Page 38 – LUMO–The Gospels for the visual age/ Lightstock | Description: The disciples on a boat

Page 41 – serpeblu/ Getty Images | Description: Ancient Roman soldier

Page 42 – kake1967/ iStock | Description: Close up of the hands of a leather craftsman

Page 45 – LUMO–The Gospels for the visual age/ Lightstock | Description: Jesus calls His first disciples

Page 46 – paulrommer/ Depositphotos | Description: Israel in watercolour

Page 49 – HisWondrousWorks/ iStock | Description: Miracle of Yahsua

Page 50 – Jan Kopřiva/Unsplash | Description: white nimbus cloud; Jason Leung/Unsplash | Description: gray rabbit on raod;
Jonathan Kemper/Unsplash | Description: black and white eagle on black wooden fence;
Kenneth Schipper Vera /Unsplash | Description: little pig; Mana5280/ Unsplash | Description: smiling hyena;
Henry Perk/ Unsplash | Description: Scallops on fishmonger counter;
Life On White/ Canva | Description: Camel; dpenn0808/ pixabay | Description: Lion

Page 52 – DesignPicsInc/ Depositphotos | Description: Jesus approaching a woman

Page 55 – LUMO–The Gospels for the visual age/ Lightstock | Description: Jesus and the miraculous catch of fish

Page 56 – sakepaint/ istockphoto | Description: White dove

Page 58 – ratpack2/Depositphotos | Description: Perseus saving Andromeda from a sea monster

Page 63 – Sesbastian Pena Lambarri/Unsplash | Description: Silver fishes underwater Maldives

Page 64 – Aaron Burden/ Unsplash| Description: School of gray fish

Page 65 – Public Domain /Wellcome Collection | Description: Jaffa, ancient Joppa, looking north. Coloured lithograph by Louis Haghe after David Roberts, 1843.

Page 66 – Daiga Ellaby/Unsplash | Description: selective focus photography of white hammock

Design, including endpapers and iconography: Beckon Creative | beckoncreative.biz

Bible Versions

Scripture quotations marked BSB are taken from the The Holy Bible, Berean Study Bible, BSB Copyright ©2016 by Bible Hub. Used by Permission. All Rights Reserved Worldwide.

Scripture quotations marked CEV are from the Contemporary English Version Copyright © 1991, 1992, 1995 by American Bible Society. Used by Permission.

Scripture quotations marked ESV are taken from the ESV® Bible (The Holy Bible, English Standard Version®), copyright © 2001 by Crossway, a publishing ministry of Good News Publishers. Used by permission. All rights reserved.

Scripture quotations marked GWT are taken from GOD'S WORD®, a copyrighted work of God's Word to the Nations. Quotations are used by permission. Copyright 1995 by God's Word to the Nations. All rights reserved.

Scripture quotations marked ISV are taken from the Holy Bible: International Standard Version®. Copyright © 1996-forever by The ISV Foundation. ALL RIGHTS RESERVED INTERNATIONALLY. Used by permission.

Scripture quotations marked KJV are taken from the King James Version of the Bible. Public domain.

Scripture quotations marked NAS are taken from the New American Standard Bible®, Copyright © 1960, 1962, 1963, 1968, 1971, 1972, 1973, 1975, 1977, 1995 by The Lockman Foundation. Used by permission. (www.Lockman.org)

Scripture quotations marked NIV are taken from the Holy Bible, New International Version®, NIV®. Copyright © 1973, 1978, 1984, 2011 by Biblica, Inc.™ Used by permission of Zondervan. All rights reserved worldwide. www.zondervan.com The "NIV" and "New International Version" are trademarks registered in the United States Patent and Trademark Office by Biblica, Inc.™.

© Anne Hamilton 2023

Published by Armour Books

P. O. Box 492, Corinda QLD 4075 AUSTRALIA

ISBN: 978-1-925380-38-5

All rights reserved. No part of this publication may be reproduced, stored in, or introduced into a retrieval system, or transmitted, in any form, or by any means (electronic, mechanical, photocopying, recording or otherwise) without the prior written permission of the publisher.

A catalogue record for this book is available from the National Library of Australia

No net less wide than a man's whole heart,
nor less fine a mesh than love,
will hold the sacred Fish.

> C.S. Lewis,
> *Reflections on the Psalms*

www.ingramcontent.com/pod-product-compliance
Lightning Source LLC
Chambersburg PA
CBHW041126130526
44590CB00054B/90